B48 764 185 7

The Olympic Games

Steve Flinders

D1386704

Oxford Bookworms
Factfiles

OXFORD UNIVERSITY PRESS 1999

Oxford University Press, Great Clarendon Street,
Oxford OX2 6DP

Oxford   New York
Athens   Auckland   Bangkok   Bogotá   Buenos Aires
Calcutta   Cape Town   Chennai   Dar es Salaam
Delhi   Florence   Hong Kong   Istanbul   Karachi
Kuala Lumpur   Madrid   Melbourne   Mexico City
Mumbai   Nairobi   Paris   São Paulo   Shanghai
Singapore   Taipei   Tokyo   Toronto   Warsaw
and associated companies in Berlin   Ibadan

OXFORD and OXFORD ENGLISH
are trade marks of Oxford University Press

ISBN 0 19 422872 X

© Oxford University Press

First published 1999
Second impression 2000

Printed in China

ACKNOWLEDGEMENTS
Allsport UK Ltd pp 9 (The Olympic torch), 11 (Fanny Blankers-
Koen), 14 (Mark Spitz), 26 (Marathon); Ancient Art and
Architecture Collection Ltd pp 2 (Chariot racing, Discobulus),
3 (Wrestling); Colorsport pp 1 (Female athletes/Andrew Cowie),
7 (Munich 1972), 9 (The Olympic flame/Andrew Cowie), 12 (Bob
Beamon), 13 (Michael Johnson/Andrew Cowie), 16 (Olga Korbut),
20 (Torvill & Dean), 25 (Wall poster), 27 (Closing ceremony/
Andrew Cowie); Corbis UK Ltd pp 4 (Baron Coubertin/Bettmann),
20 (Jean-Claude Killy/Bettmann), 21 (Eric Heiden/Bettmann);
Hulton Getty Picture Collection p 5 (Diving display); PA News
Photolibrary pp 5 (Paris 1900), 18 (Chris Boardman); International
Olympic Committee p 6 (Olympic logo); Popperfoto pp 2
(Leonidas), 4 (100 metres race), 6 (Medal ceremony 1968),
8 (Olympic flag, Centennial opening ceremony), 10 (Jesse Owens),
11 (Emil Zátopek), 12 (Dick Fosbury, Carl Lewis), 13 (Florence
Griffith-Joyner), 14 (Dawn Frazer, Water polo/Brunskill, Johnny
Weissmuller), 15 (Mingxia Fu/Reuters), 17 (Cassius Clay),
18 ('Magic' Johnson), 19 (Synchronized swimming, Shooting/
Reuters), 21 (Matti Nykanen), 23 (wheelchair race/Brunskill,
Yachting/J. Prevost), 24 (Ben Johnson/Brunskill), 25 (IOC members/
Reuters); Rex Features pp 22 (face painting/ firework display),
17 (Oddjob); Topham Picturepoint p 17 (Piero D'Inzeo).

OXFORD BOOKWORMS

For a full list of titles in all the Oxford Bookworms
series, please refer to the Oxford English catalogue.

Oxford Bookworms Factfiles
Original readers giving varied and interesting
information about a range of non-fiction topics.
Titles available include:

STAGE 1   (400 HEADWORDS)
Animals in Danger
Diana, Princess of Wales
Flight
Kings and Queens of Britain
London
New York
Scotland
Titanic

STAGE 2   (700 HEADWORDS)
Football
Forty Years of Pop
Ireland
Oxford
Pollution
Rainforests
Seasons and Celebrations
UFOs
Under the Ground

STAGE 3   (1000 HEADWORDS)
Australia and New Zealand
The Cinema
The Olympic Games
Recycling
The USA

STAGE 4   (1400 HEADWORDS)
Disaster!
Great Crimes

Oxford Bookworms Library
Original stories and adaptations of classic and
modern fiction.

Oxford Bookworms Playscripts
Original plays and adaptations of classic and modern
drama.

Oxford Bookworms Collection
Fiction by well known classic and modern authors.
Texts are not abridged or simplified in any way.

1 Welcome to the Olympics

Every four years since 1896, except during times of war, the best sportsmen and sportswomen in the world have met together for the Olympic Games. In 1896 – the first of the modern Olympics – two hundred athletes from fourteen countries tried to win medals in forty-three events. In the Games of today, there are more than ten thousand athletes from nearly two hundred countries for nearly three hundred events. Then there were nine sports. Now there are more than twenty-five.

The Olympic Games is the greatest sports meeting in the world. It brings together people from almost every country and from many sports in a way that no other competition does. Being at the Olympics is the life's dream for thousands of athletes; winning an Olympic medal is their highest goal.

Some people think that the Olympics today are too big, or that money is too important in the Olympics. Many do not like the way Olympic cities are chosen. Some people just hate sport. But most people love the Games – the excitement, the danger, and the athletes who, in the words of the Olympic motto, are 'faster, higher, stronger'.

In this book we will look at the past, the present and the future of the Olympics.

2 The ancient Olympics

The first Olympians were gods. The Greeks who lived 3,000 years ago told stories about the competitions between the gods on the mountain of Olympus in northern Greece. The word *Olympic* comes from here – and from the town of Olympia where the Greeks began to have games as a way of giving thanks to their gods.

Leonidas

The Greeks loved sports and games, and held them in many different places, but the Olympic Games finally became the most important. These Games were for Zeus, their most important god.

The first Olympics which we are sure about were in 776 BC, but they probably started a long time before this. The Games became very important. Wars stopped while

Throwing the discus

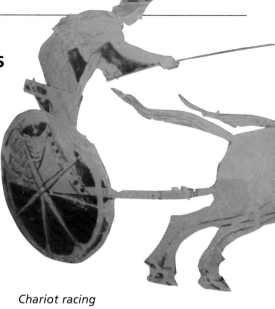

Chariot racing

the Games were on. People then were just as crazy about sport as they are now and they came a very long way to watch: the stadium at Olympia could hold 20,000 people. The athletes were often from rich families and were very serious about sport, too. They came from all over the Greek world, but foreigners could not compete, and women could not even watch: partly because the athletes did not wear clothes. The athletes did

not get medals, they won crowns of leaves. The idea was to compete because you loved sport, not because you wanted money. But in fact, like today, the winners often became very rich and famous, and their cities became famous too.

Like today, the Games were every four years. At first there was only one event, a running race of just under 200 metres called the *stade*. Then a two stade race was introduced. In 720 BC, another race of about 4.5 kilometres was added. Then came horse riding, chariot racing, wrestling and other events. One Olympic winner was Leonidas of Rhodes. Between 164 and 152 BC, he won all three running events in four different Games: twelve wins! – the most successful Olympic athlete of all time.

The Ancient Games had some of the same problems as the modern ones. As time passed, more and more Olympic athletes became professionals and some of them tried to win unfairly. In AD 67, when the Emperor Nero decided to enter the Olympic chariot race, he was the only competitor, because everyone was afraid of him. So he became an Olympic champion even though he had had too much to drink and did not finish the race! In AD 393 the Emperor Theodosius stopped the Games. It was more than a thousand years since the first Olympics, but soon the Olympics were forgotten, and it would be more than a thousand years before the next Olympics happened.

Greek wrestling

3 The modern Olympics are born

The Greeks gave us the Olympics, but it was a Frenchman who gave us the modern Games. Pierre de Coubertin (1863–1937) was interested in the ancient Greeks and their ideas about the importance of a healthy mind in a healthy body. He came to believe that sport should be an important part of what everyone learns. He believed that sport could make everyone a better person, and that people should do sport for love, not money. He

Pierre de Coubertin

believed that the most important thing in sport is not to win, but just to do it. These were the ideas behind the first Games of modern times, held in Athens in 1896.

The Greeks loved the Games and made it a great success. 1896 was the seventy-fifth birthday of their country and they were happy to have this important competition in their capital city: forty thousand people watched the opening ceremony in the new Olympic stadium.

The start of the 100 metres at Athens, 1896

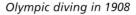

Olympic diving in 1908

Olympic rowing in 1908

The Olympics were very different then from now. Most of the two hundred men who took part in those first Games were Greek, although some (mostly rich) foreigners were also there. There were no women. Today it takes years to get to the Olympics – years of hard work, problems and difficulties – all for a race which could take less than a minute. But a hundred years ago, the Olympians were part-time, not full-time athletes, amateurs not professionals (although they did accept prizes). The Olympics have come a long way since Athens.

Some funny things happened in the early Games. In Athens, some of the athletes were there only because they were on holiday. A cyclist won a medal after he borrowed a bicycle from someone in the crowd. The swimming events were not in a swimming pool but in the sea – it was very cold! – and in Paris in 1900, they were in the River Seine. And in the rowing in Paris, two Dutchmen needed someone to make their boat go the right way, and asked a small boy, between seven and ten years old, to help them. He won a gold medal – the youngest ever gold medallist – but no-one ever knew his name.

4 From Athens to Athens

Stockholm Helsinki
1912, 1956 1952
Amsterdam
1928
London   Berlin *1936*
1908, 1948   • Moscow *1980*
St Louis   Paris •   Antwerp *1920*
1904 Montreal   *1900, 1924* • Munich *1972*
   1976   Rome *1960*
Los Angeles • Atlanta   Barcelona Athens
1932, 1984 *1996*   *1992* *1896, 2004*
Mexico City
1968

Seoul
1988

Tokyo
1964

Sydney
2000

Melbourne •
1956

Chamonix in France (see page 20). In 1928, at Amsterdam, women competed in the athletics for the first time (see page 10). It had not been easy for women at the Olympics. None of the people who started the Olympic Games in the 1890s with Pierre de Coubertin were women. There were no women athletes at the first Olympics and although some women

From the first Olympiad in Athens in 1896 to the twenty-eighth Olympiad in Athens in 2004, the story of the Olympic Games has not always been a happy one. After 1896, the next two Games were not so successful and it was not sure that the Games would continue. But by the 1920s the Games had become famous and getting ready for them was serious – as you can see from the film *Chariots of Fire* about the 1924 Games in Paris. It was also in this year that the first Winter Olympics were held in

Mexico 1968: Tommy Smith and John Carlos show their support for black power

were at the second Games in Paris in 1900, the International Olympic Committee (IOC) did not want women there: the first real Olympic medals for women were not until 1912, in swimming. Women's athletics started in 1928 but they could not run more than 200 metres until 1960! Even in 1984, at Los Angeles, there were still no 5,000 or 10,000 metre races for women. The first women did not join the IOC until 1981: and there are still many more men than women on the IOC today. Sport is still a man's world.

There were problems in Berlin in 1936. Hitler wanted to show the world that the best athletes were white. He got very angry when a young black American athlete called Jesse Owens won four gold medals. The Games of 1940 and 1944 did not happen because of the Second World War. The 1956 Games in Melbourne were the first outside Europe or the USA, and in 1964 the Games went to Asia for the first time – to Tokyo. In 1968 in Mexico City, Tommy Smith and John Carlos showed their support for black power: they were sent home immediately. And the Mexican police

had big fights with students before the Games. In 1972, eleven Israeli athletes were killed by terrorists in the Olympic Village where the athletes live. The terrorists were killed by police.

In 1980, only eighty countries went to the Moscow Games because the Russian army had entered Afghanistan: once again it seemed possible that the Olympic Games would not go on. In 1984, the Russians and some other countries did not go to Los Angeles. But, although there have been problems, the Games have continued. 169 countries went to the 1992 Games in Barcelona which were happy and very successful.

Flags at half-mast after the deaths of eleven Israeli athletes, Munich 1972

5 Going to the Olympics

The five circles of the Olympic flag: one for each continent

The Olympic opening ceremony, Atlanta 1996

It is not easy to be an Olympian. If you want to be one in eight or twelve years' time, you must decide now to give those years to your sport. If you can do this, then perhaps one day you will join the world's best athletes in the Olympic stadium for the opening ceremony of the Olympic Games. The athletes who are there have worked hard for this moment. They have worked so hard that often their bodies hurt. Sometimes they felt so tired that they wanted to stop the endless work. But they always made themselves go on, and they told themselves that one day they would be the best.

For the opening ceremony, the competitors begin by entering the main stadium and then walk round, country by country, the Greek team first, the home country last. There is singing and dancing from the people of the Olympic city. The leader of the home country talks to the people in the stadium and, through television, to millions of people around the world, and then the President of the IOC talks as well. The Olympic flag goes up. Now a runner enters the Olympic stadium carrying a lighted torch. The flame he or she carries was lit by the sun on Mount Olympus, and has been carried by different runners from there to the beginning of another Olympic Games.

None of the athletes knows what will happen during the next two weeks. Some will know the happiest moments in their whole lives, others will know the saddest, many will know the most difficult. None of them will ever forget this time. A few hundred out of the ten thousand there at the start of the Olympics will know the special excitement and happiness which comes to the medal winners: their dreams really have come true. From now on they are special people for always.

A runner enters the stadium carrying the Olympic torch

The flame burns over the stadium for the two weeks of the Games

Olympic city. The runner runs up the steps to light the flame, which will burn during the two weeks of the Games. Birds fly up from the stadium. An athlete (sometimes two – a man and a woman) makes the Olympic promise to play fairly, in front of all the others. It is the

6 Olympic athletics

When they think of the Olympics, most people think first of athletics, one of the few sports which has been part of every Olympic Games since the beginning. It is also the biggest Olympic sport. Athletics happens either on the track – walking and running events – or on the field – jumping and throwing events. Here are just a few of the great track and field stars of the modern Olympics.

Paris 1924. **Paavo Nurmi** of Finland won five gold medals in six days, two of them within one hour! His special events were the 1,500 metres, the 5,000 metres and the 10,000 metres. He learnt to run in the forests of Finland, summer and winter; he never ate meat and never drank tea or coffee. His Olympic total was nine golds and three silvers in the Games of 1920, 1924 and 1928 from seven different events. During his life as a runner, he broke twenty-nine world records in sixteen events. Nurmi was one of the first, and one of the greatest, of the many 'Flying Finns' to win at the Olympics.

Berlin 1936. One afternoon in 1935, **Jesse Owens** of the USA had

Jesse Owens, the star of the Berlin Games, made Hitler angry

broken six world records in less than an hour! At the Berlin Olympics, he was the star. He won four gold medals in the 100 metres, 200 metres, 4 x 100 metre relay and the long jump: he was the first man to jump over eight metres and his world record stood for twenty-five years. Owens came from a poor black family: he was one of eleven children. People will always remember him as the runner who showed, through the beauty and greatness of his running, that Hitler's ideas were wrong. In the 1984 Games at Los Angeles, his granddaughter carried the Olympic flame into the stadium.

London 1948. Because of the war, **Fanny Blankers-Koen** of Holland was already thirty when she got her first chance to go to the Olympics. People said she was too old. In eight days in London, she ran eleven races and won them all. She won four golds in the 100 metres, the 200 metres, the 80 metre hurdles and the 4 x 100 metre relay. People saw that Fanny was a great athlete, and they began to take women's athletics more seriously.

Helsinki 1952. **Emil Zátopek** of Czechoslovakia changed long distance running for always, because of all the hard work he had done to get ready for the Games. Sometimes he ran with his wife (also a gold medallist) on his back to get stronger for races. He had already won Olympic gold in 1948 in the 10,000 metres. Now he won three more gold medals, in the 5,000 metres, the 10,000 metres and the marathon. No-one had ever won these three long races in the same Olympics before, and no-one has done it since.

Fanny Blankers-Koen (right) made people take women's athletics seriously

In Helsinki, he broke the world marathon record by six minutes – and it was the first marathon he had ever run! From 1948 to 1954, he was unbeaten in thirty-eight races over 10,000 metres. Zátopek is easy to see in photographs because his face always seems to show so much pain. Someone said he looked as if he had been knifed in the heart. But he was *the* distance

Emil Zátopek of Czechoslovakia, the long distance king

runner of the 1952 Games and of the 1950s.

Mexico City 1968. Two American field athletes were among the stars of Mexico. Before **Bob Beamon**'s first long jump, the world record had been 8.12 metres, not much more than Jesse Owens' Berlin record of 8.06 metres, made thirty-one years before. In one jump – no-one who saw it will ever forget it – Beamon

Mexico City 1968: Bob Beamon jumps into the record books

Carl Lewis: the greatest

Dick Fosbury doing the Flop

added 78 centimetres to the record! The Olympic record still stands. At the same Games, **Dick Fosbury** took the Olympic high jump record from 2.18 to 2.24 metres by jumping in a new way: head-first and onto his back. It looked as if he would break his neck, but now every high jumper does the 'Fosbury Flop'.

Los Angeles 1984. **Carl Lewis** (USA) won four golds in a single Games, and in the same events as Jesse Owens – the 100 metres, 200 metres, long jump and 4 x 100 metre relay. In

1988 in Seoul, he won the 100 metres again – the first Olympian to do this; and he won the long jump; and the silver in the 200 metres. At the same Games, a black American woman, **Florence Griffith-Joyner** ('Flo-Jo') won three golds in the 100 metres, 200 metres (with a new world record of 21.34) and 4 x 100 metre relay, and a silver in the 4 x 400 metre relay. In 1992 in Barcelona, Lewis won the long jump again and another gold in the relay. In 1996 in Atlanta, he won the long jump again: he had won the long jump at every Games from 1984 to 1996! Four Olympic Games, nine golds and one silver. Lewis is the greatest Olympic athlete of modern times.

Atlanta 1996. **Michael Johnson** of the USA won a gold medal in the 200 metres in a world record time of 19.32 seconds: the specialists had thought that no-one would run this fast until the middle of the twenty-first century! The times of the races were

Flo-Jo going for gold at Seoul

changed so that he could compete in the 400 metres, and he won a second gold in this too, the first man to win these two events in the same Games.

The time when a runner is at the top is short – usually just a few years: even the great athletes usually have the chance to shine in only one Games, sometimes two, or very unusually, like Carl Lewis, three or four. But every athlete will remember the Olympics for his or her lifetime, and the books and the films can keep alive what they did, for the rest of us, for always.

Michael Johnson: the star of Atlanta

7 In the swimming pool

Johnny Weismuller –
first Olympic swimmer under a minute

There was no swimming in the ancient Olympics, but swimming has always been part of the modern Games, and it is the second biggest Olympic sport. The first 50 metre pool was used in 1924, the first pool inside was used in 1948. Now the pools are always very modern, and the races can be timed to 0.001 seconds. The USA has always been strong in swimming: it has won more than thirty per cent of all Olympic swimming medals since 1896. Here are just a few of the great stars.

Dawn Frazer –
100 metre freestyle champion three times

Johnny Weismuller of the USA was the first man to swim 100 metres in under sixty seconds. (Now the men's Olympic record is Matt Biondi's 48.63 – see page 15.) He won five gold medals in the Games of 1924 and 1928 and later became the star of the Tarzan films.

Like Jesse Owens,

Water polo, Barcelona 1992:
Italy beat Spain in extra time

Mark Spitz – the most successful
Olympic swimmer of all time

Dawn Frazer of Australia came from a large family – she was the youngest of eight children. She was the swimming star of the 1956 Games in front of her home crowd in Melbourne, and is the only swimmer, man or woman, to win the 100 metres freestyle three times (in 1956, 1960 and 1964). Her medals total was four golds and four silvers.

The USA's **Mark Spitz** is the most successful Olympic swimmer of all time. In Mexico City in 1968 he won two golds, one silver and one bronze, but that was just the beginning. In Munich in 1972 he won seven gold medals – a record number in one Games – in the 100 metre and 200 metre freestyle, the 100 metre and 200 metre butterfly, and the 4 x 100 metre, 4 x 200 metre and 4 x 400 metre relays. In Seoul in 1988, **Matt Biondi** (USA) was the swimming star with five golds, one silver and one bronze. Between 1988 and 1992, he had won eight golds, two silvers and a bronze.

Swimming is not the only Olympic sport in the swimming pool. **Water polo** is hard, fast and exciting. It is a game of four seven-minute quarters, but extra time is played when both teams have the same number of goals. The longest Olympic water polo final was won by Italy against Spain, in 1992, when Italy got a goal just before the end of the sixth period of extra time!

And there is **diving** which is very beautiful to watch. One of the diving events is from 10 metres above the pool, the same as diving from the top of a house! Greg Louganis of the USA won both men's golds in 1984 and again, after hitting his head very badly early in the Games, in 1988. Mingxia Fu of China won both diving golds in Barcelona when she was only thirteen. She won them again in Atlanta four years later.

Atlanta 1996: Mingxia Fu wins again

8 Other Olympic sports

There are now nearly thirty Olympic sports. Some sports come and go, but many have been in the Games for a long time.

Together with athletics and swimming, **gymnastics** is probably the most popular sport at the Olympics. It was also a sport of the ancient Games. And one person who did more than any other to make gymnastics popular was the Russian, Olga Korbut, who became a very big star when she won two golds and a silver at the 1972 Games, and brought gymnastics into the lives of millions for the first time. Another Russian gymnast, Larissa Latynina, holds the record for the most golds in any sport – nine – and the most medals – eighteen – which she won between 1956 and 1964.

More than twenty Olympic **boxing** winners have gone on to become professional world champions. The most famous of these was Cassius Clay, an Olympic champion in 1960, who later changed his name to Muhammad Ali and became probably the best-known and the best-loved sportsman in the world. Ali later threw away the gold medal which he had won for the USA, because he believed that the US government was not fair to black people.

Although amateur boxing is safer than professional boxing, many people believe that it is too dangerous, and should not be an

Olga Korbut brought gymnastics to millions

Cassius Clay (Muhammad Ali), Olympic boxing champion, Rome 1960

Piero d'Inzeo rode in eight different Games

Olympic sport. Ali became very ill, probably because of his boxing. When the Olympic Games came to Atlanta in 1996, Ali carried the Olympic torch at the opening of the Games, one of the pictures of the Atlanta Games which people will remember most.

Many other champions have been made famous by their medals. Harold Sakata of the USA won a silver medal in **weightlifting** in 1948. Later he starred as Oddjob in the James Bond film, *Goldfinger*.

Equestrianism is an ancient as well as a modern Olympic sport. The three events with horses are the only ones at the Games with animals. It is one of the two Olympic sports in which women compete with men for the same medals (the other is yachting). When the Games went to Melbourne in 1956, the equestrian events had to be in Stockholm because foreign horses were not let into Australia. The record for the most Games is held by two Italian brothers, Raimondo and Piero

Harold Sakata (Oddjob), weightlifter and film star

d'Inzeo, who were both at eight Olympics between 1948 and 1976.

Professionals can now play Olympic **football** but they must be under twenty-three and must not have played in the football World Cup: in 1992 Spain beat Poland 3–2 to win gold in front of a football-crazy home crowd of 92,000. Olympic **tennis** and

Barcelona 1992: Earvin 'Magic' Johnson of the USA's first Olympic 'Dream Team'

Barcelona 1992: Chris Boardman changed the sport of cycling

basketball players can also be professional now. The US 'Dream Team' of top professional basketball players was let into the Games in 1992, and has won every gold medal since.

Technology is changing some sports. **Cycling** today is very different from the past. Chris Boardman of Great Britain changed cycling for always when he won the 4,000 metres individual gold medal with his new bicycle in 1992 in Barcelona. Was it the man or the machine which won the medal? Top cyclists can now go at more than 70 kilometres per hour. **Shooting** is another hi-tech sport which has changed very much over the last hundred years.

There are also some very strange sports at the Olympics. **Synchronized swimming** is a kind of dancing in water. It is difficult to say what a sport is, but many people feel that this is not a sport and should not be in the Games. There are questions about some other sports as well. **Baseball** is not played in many

Shooting: another hi-tech sport

countries: there were only eight baseball teams in Atlanta. **Taekwondo** also is not known in most parts of the world, and is much less popular than karate, which is not an Olympic sport.

Synchronized swimming: is it really a sport?

9 The Winter Olympics

From 1924 to 1992, the Winter
Olympics were held in the same year
as the Summer Games. But since the
Lillehammer Games of 1994 they
have been *between* Summer Games.
Like the Summer Olympics, the
Winter Olympics have got bigger.
There were 294 competitors at the
first Winter Olympics at Chamonix.
Today there are nearly 2,000. In
1924 there were thirteen events; now
there are more than sixty. You do not
need a big city for the Winter
Olympics: Lillehammer has only
21,000 people. But there is one other
thing which you must have:
snow! All the Winter sports
are played on snow or ice,
but at Cortina d'Ampezzo
in 1956, it did not snow

Alpine skiing: Jean-Claude Killy

before the Games, so the Italians had
to move snow down the mountain.
Then, on the day of the opening
ceremony, it snowed a lot and they
had to move most of it away again.
Innsbruck (1964) and Lake Placid
(1980) had the same
problems. The right

*Torvill and Deane
won gold for their
ice dancing in
Sarajevo*

weather is very important for the Winter Olympics!

The Winter Olympics are exciting. There is downhill (or Alpine) skiing and cross country (or Nordic) skiing, ski jumping, skating, and many more events. Here are just a few of the many stars of the Winter Olympics.

People called the 1968 Games in Grenoble the 'Killympics' because **Jean-Claude Killy** of France won three Alpine men's gold medals, in the Downhill, Slalom and Giant Slalom, in front of a home crowd. Killy did much to bring the Winter Olympics back to France in 1992 to Albertville, and these Games were also successful, although some people were unhappy about where some of the building was done. The Norwegians were very careful not to cut down too many trees and not to do too much building in Lillehammer two years later.

Jayne Torvill and Christopher Deane of Great Britain changed figure skating with their ice dancing at Sarajevo in 1984, and won gold. Sadly, the places where the Games happened were later destroyed by war. Ten years after, there was a minute's silence

Matti Nykaenen of Finland – four ski jumping golds in 1984 and 1988

during the opening ceremony of the Lillehammer Games to remember the people of Sarajevo. Part of the Olympic idea is to bring peace through sport and friendship.

Speed skating: Eric Heiden (USA) won five golds in 1980

10 'We have the Games!'

'We have the Games!' Sydney people are happy to hear that the 2000 Games will go to Sydney

Many cities try very hard to have the Olympic Games. They believe that the Games will make their city famous and bring in money and people. Sometimes this is true: for Barcelona, for example. But sometimes it is not: Montreal (1976) lost a lot of money and the city had money problems for many years after.

It takes six to ten years to get ready for the Olympic Games. Would you like them in your city? Let's see if you have what you need for a future Summer Games.

Your city must not be too small. You probably need a city of at least two million people, and they must want the Games: visitors will want a warm welcome. You need about 40,000 unpaid helpers and if they do not speak English, you must teach them. You must also be ready for two Olympics, not one, because after the Olympics comes the Paralympics for handicapped people.

Your city must not be too high. Some athletes had problems in Mexico City in 1968, because, at 2,240 metres above the sea their bodies could not get enough air. The air must also be clean and you must have good weather: people want a warm and sunny Olympics. Your ideas for the Games must be good for the environment.

It must be easy to get to your city by plane. Inside the city there must be good roads, good trains and lots of buses to move people from one place to another. In Atlanta in 1996, the buses were bad and people got angry.

You must have good places for sport: you must already have most of the stadiums and swimming pools you will need, because it will be too expensive to build new ones. They must not be too far from one another.

You need the sea for yachting (Barcelona 1992)

The sea should be near for the yachting.

You need about 300,000 beds as well as lots of places for your three million visitors to eat. 10,000 athletes will stay in the Olympic Village and 15,000 media people will come for the Games (more than the athletes!) You must have good telephones and good computers so that the media people can tell the world about your Games.

You must know how to do big sports competitions. Your country must be safe for visitors.

And you must know how to get the 1.5 billion dollars you need for the Games. Finally you must work very hard and spend a lot of money to tell the old men of the IOC that your city is the best.

If they agree, then you need good weather, some luck, clever people who will work without sleep for two weeks to make everyone happy, and then you will have a good Games. Good luck!

Not one Olympics but two: after the Olympics, the Paralympics

11 Olympic problems

The Games are always changing, and not everyone thinks that the changes are good ones.

The first major problem is money. When Baron de Coubertin started the Olympics, he believed that only amateurs should go there. Now, some Olympic sports are open to professionals, others are not. In most sports it is very difficult for athletes who do not work full-time at their sport to win medals. And people want athletes to do better and better all the time.

So some athletes cheat, usually by taking drugs. Ben Johnson of Canada came first in the 100 metres in Seoul in 1988, but after the race, Olympic doctors found drugs in his body, and the gold medal was given to Carl Lewis, who had come second. Johnson was stopped from running in international competition for two years. He had been the fastest man in the world for just two days. Since 1988 there have been a lot more drugs checks on athletes. But sometimes they are told by their countries to take drugs: some Chinese swimmers who broke world records

Ben Johnson

in the 1990s did this. It can be difficult to tell when athletes have taken some drugs, but the IOC could do more to stop drug taking at the Olympics.

Money is important for the athletes but also for the city where the Games are happening. The Games are very expensive. Who will pay? Money comes from selling tickets (eleven million in Atlanta). The cities themselves also pay a lot; sometimes money comes from the government, too. But all this is not enough. The IOC's answer is to sell the Games. Big companies like Coca-Cola and McDonald's give money to the IOC so that Coca-Cola can be the Olympic

The Olympics are also about selling

The IOC: who chooses them?

drink, and McDonald's the Olympic food. NBC, the American TV company, has given money to the IOC to be the Olympic TV company until the year 2008. NBC chooses what people see on their televisions, and even tries to decide when the races will be, so that Americans can watch them live. Is there a better way to decide this?

Some people think that the Games have become more about selling than about sport. Is there another way to pay for the Games?

The last big question is: Who runs the Olympics? The ninety or more people on the International Olympic Committee choose the Olympic cities, own and sell the logo, and decide which sports should be Olympic sports. But many of them are more than seventy years old, and it is not easy to see how they get on the committee, or why they stay so long. In 1999, six men had to leave the IOC because they had taken money and presents from cities which wanted the Games. In the twenty-first century, the IOC must be more open and more honest, it must have younger people, it must do something about money and drugs and must make sport more important than selling.

12 The future of the Olympics

The last event of the Games is the men's marathon. It is 42.195 kilometres long (the first marathon runner, Pheidippedes, ran 280 kilometres to tell the people of Athens that their army had won the battle of Marathon: he dropped dead after giving them the news). The athletes run for more than two hours through the streets of the city and finish by running once round the stadium.

After the men's marathon comes the closing ceremony, watched by a stadium full of people and a television audience of more than three billion – more than half of all the people in the world. Again there is singing and dancing, but this time the athletes can sing and dance too: they have all finished what they came to do, so they too can take it easy. This is the beginning of one big night-long party before the journey home the next day.

It is the end of the Games and time to think about the future of the Olympics. Where are the Olympic Games going?

Some people say that the Olympics are too big. There

The last event of the Games: the men's marathon

are now more than 270 events, double the number in the 1950s, six times the number in 1896. The Games get bigger and so more expensive to organize. So money becomes more important and people worry that the old Olympic ideas of Pierre de Coubertin are being lost.

Perhaps there should be fewer sports, especially in professional sports which already have their own world competitions. Football lovers are more interested in the football World Cup than in Olympic football. Tennis players want to win at Wimbledon more than an Olympic medal. Should the rich men of the US professional basketball team play at the Olympics? Perhaps these should not be Olympic sports. But then, swimming and athletics also have their own World Championships and an Olympics without swimming and athletics would not really be an Olympics at all.

Which sports should be in the Olympics of the future? Will people lose interest as it becomes more and more difficult to break world records? Will new technology kill some sports? Will money and drugs kill the Olympics? Will the Olympics die?

No. There may be problems but the feelings of most people for the Games are as strong as ever. Sport is a language that most people can understand, and there is something special about the Olympics. The big number of different sports makes it different. Friendships are made not just between athletes from different countries but also from different sports. More countries are winning medals and more countries are winning golds than ever before. And in most sports, the gold medal is still the final, the greatest, the best prize to win. The Olympic Games have changed a lot, and will continue to change, but there will never be an Olympic Games without surprises: they are still the greatest show on earth.

*The closing ceremony:
now all the athletes can relax*

Exercises

A Checking your understanding

Pages 1–5 *Write answers to these questions*
1 When and where was the first modern Olympic Games?
2 How many athletes took part?
3 How many Olympic sports are there today?
4 How many events are there today?
5 When were the first ancient Olympics which we are sure about?
6 Who is the most successful Olympic athlete of all time, and why?
7 What was the first Olympic event, and what was its name?
8 Who gave us the modern Olympic Games?
9 Who was the youngest ever gold medallist?

Pages 6–9 *How much can you remember? Check your answers.*
1 Where were the first Winter Olympics held?
2 When and where did women compete in the Olympics for the first time?
3 Why did Hitler get angry in Berlin in 1936?
4 When and where were the first Games outside Europe?
5 How many countries went to the Moscow Games of 1980?
6 How many countries went to the Barcelona Games of 1992?

Pages 10–21 *Are these sentences true (T) or false (F)?*
1 Paavo Nurmi never drank tea or coffee.
2 Jesse Owens had ten brothers and sisters.
3 Fanny Blankers-Koen won four gold medals in Helsinki in 1952.
4 Carl Lewis won medals at five different Olympic Games.
5 Dawn Frazer won gold in the 100 metre freestyle three times.
6 Mark Spitz won seven golds in Mexico in 1968.
7 Olga Korbut holds the record for the most gold medals in any sport.
8 Muhammad Ali carried the torch at the Atlanta Olympics in 1996.
9 The Winter Olympics is now in the same year as the Summer Olympics.

B Working with language

1 *Complete these sentences with information from pages 22 and 23.*
   1 You must also be ready for two Olympics, not one, because . . .
   2 Some athletes had problems in Mexico City in 1968 because . . .
   3 In Atlanta in 1996, the buses . . .
   4 You must already have most of the stadiums and swimming pools you need because . .
   5 You must have good telephones and good computers so that . . .

2 *Put these sentences into the right order. Then check your order on page 24.*
   1 In most sports it is very difficult for athletes who do not work full-time at their sport to win medals.
   2 The first major problem is money.
   3 When Baron de Coubertin started the Olympics he believed that only amateurs should go there.
   4 So some athletes cheat, usually by taking drugs.
   5 Now some Olympic sports are open to professionals, others are not.
   6 And people want athletes to do better and better all the time.

C Activities

1 You are a member of the International Olympic Committee. What changes do you want to make to the next Olympic Games? What new sports would you like to see there?
2 You work for a newspaper. You can talk to any of the athletes in this book. Write down your questions and the athlete's answers.

D Project work

Write **either** the story of one Olympic sport **or** the story of your country and the Olympics (choose the Winter or the Summer Olympics).

Glossary

amateur a person who does not take money for doing a sport

ancient very old, belonging to times which are long past

artificial not natural, man-made

athlete a sportsman or sportswoman

champion a winner

championship a sports meeting to decide who are the champions

compete to try to win something

crown a king or queen wears this on the head

distance a long distance runner runs a long way, for example 5,000 metres or 10,000 metres

drug a dangerous thing which some athletes put into their bodies to help them do their sport better

emperor an important leader

environment the world around us

event the 100 metres, the 200 metres and the 400 metres are three different events in athletics

final a lot of athletes start in an event but only the best get to the final

god the Greeks believed that gods lived for ever and controlled the world and people's lives

government the people who run a country

leader a person who tells other people what to do

logo a letter (like the big yellow 'M' for McDonald's), word or picture which a company uses in advertising

media television, newspapers, etc.

period a time period is a number of minutes for one part of a game

practise to do something again and again so that you get better

prize what the champion wins

professional a person who gets money for doing a sport

race a competition to see which athlete or team can go fastest

record when athletes do better than anyone before they make a record

relay a race for a team of, for example, runners or swimmers

team the people who play together in a game (in many games two teams play against each other)

technology ways of doing things with machines

terrorists people who use violence to try to make a government do what they want

war when countries fight each other